Finley the Fuzz

Written by Andrew Tolan
Illustrated by Juan Mont

RUNAWAY CART PUBLISHING

Copyright © 2016 by Andrew Tolan & Juan Carlos Mont.

All rights reserved. No part of this publication may be reproduced, distributed or transmitted in any form or by any means, including photocopying, recording, or other electronic or mechanical methods, without the prior written permission of the publisher, except in the case of brief quotations embodied in critical reviews and certain other noncommercial uses permitted by copyright law. For permission requests, write to the publisher at the address below.

Andrew Tolan/Runaway Cart Publishing
620 Madison St
Hoboken, New Jersey/07030

Publisher's Note: This is a work of fiction. Names, characters, places, and incidents are a product of the author's imagination. Locales and public names are sometimes used for atmospheric purposes. Any resemblance to actual people, living or dead, or to businesses, companies, events, institutions, or locales is completely coincidental.

Finley The Fuzz/ Andrew Tolan. -- 1st ed.
ISBN 978-0-9909033-5-2

Finley would like to thank Mike Ocasio. Without Mike's childlike heart, his creative eye, and professional advice, Finley wouldn't be the cool and confident little fuzz he is today.
- www.mikeocasio.com

A big thanks as well to Yader Fonseca for the big help!
- www.yaderfonseca.com

"There is no one alive who is you-er than you!"

-Dr. Seuss

Finley is a
friendly creature,
full of fuzz.

But did not
know of what
he was.

No clear sign from what
he could see,
But knew at least what
he wished he could be.

Something much different, where he could belong.
Like a bird that soars and chirps a song.
He could be perched with the other
birds up in the tree,

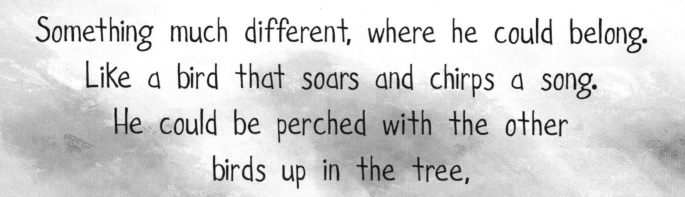

Or he could be something else entirely.

He could be smooth and springy,
like a frog.

Hopping and swimming with toads
around the bog,

Sitting on lily pads
and catching flies.

Or perhaps
he could be something
much grander in size.

Gigantic, powerful,
and certainly bold.
Like a great big polar
bear out in the cold

Slipping and sliding
all over the frosty ice.

Having fun with the other bears
would surely be nice!

Like a ferocious lion
with a mane that's hairy.

Gathering with other wild cats to let out a roar.

Then maybe he wouldn't have
to be just a fuzz anymore.

Yet a fuzz is indeed all that
Finley was,
But there are no others that
fuzz like he does.

Finley was the greatest fuzz that ever fuzzed

Because he was the only fuzz there ever was!

And though a fuzz
he thought he no longer
wanted to be,

Finley was finally able to see

There was no reason for a new
life to seek,

For being a fuzz is what makes
him unique!

Because some creatures

can swim,

and some can soar.

Some creatures can run,
while others can roar.

Some creatures can bounce,
and some can buzz,
But none can be a friendly
little fuzz!

A fuzz Finley was, and
that's all he could be.
And there was no shame
in that he now believed.

Because no other creature
could quite exactly be
A one of a kind fuzz like...

Made in the USA
Monee, IL
16 November 2022

17895626R00024